Francis Frith's
EAST ANGLIA

PHOTOGRAPHIC MEMORIES

Francis Frith's
EAST ANGLIA

◆

Clive Tully

FRITH
BOOK CO

First published in the United Kingdom in 1999 by
Frith Book Company Ltd

Text and Design copyright © Frith Book Company Ltd
Photographs copyright © The Francis Frith Collection

British Library Cataloguing in Publication Data

East Anglia
Clive Tully
ISBN 1-85937-059-4

Frith Book Company Ltd
Frith's Barn, Teffont,
Salisbury, Wiltshire SP3 5QP
Tel: +44 (0) 1722 716 376
Email: frithbook.co.uk

Printed and bound in Great Britain

CONTENTS

◆

FRANCIS FRITH: *Victorian Pioneer*

FRANCIS FRITH, Victorian founder of the world-famous photographic archive, was a complex and multitudinous man. A devout Quaker and a highly successful Victorian businessman, he was both philosophic by nature and pioneering in outlook.

By 1855 Francis Frith had already established a wholesale grocery business in Liverpool, and sold it for the astonishing sum of £200,000, which is the equivalent today of over £15,000,000. Now a multi-millionaire, he was able to indulge his passion for travel. As a child he had pored over travel books written by early explorers, and his fancy and imagination had been stirred by family holidays to the sublime mountain regions of Wales and Scotland. 'What a land of spirit-stirring and enriching scenes and places!' he had written. He was to return to these scenes of grandeur in later years to 'recapture the thousands of vivid and tender memories', but with a different purpose. Now in his thirties, and captivated by the new science of photography, Frith set out on a series of pioneering journeys to the Nile regions that occupied him from 1856 until 1860.

INTRIGUE AND ADVENTURE

He took with him on his travels a specially-designed wicker carriage that acted as both dark-room and sleeping chamber. These far-flung journeys were packed with intrigue and adventure. In his life story, written when he was sixty-three, Frith tells of being held captive by bandits, and of fighting 'an awful midnight battle to the very point of surrender with a deadly pack of hungry, wild dogs'. Sporting flowing Arab costume, Frith arrived at Akaba by camel seventy years before Lawrence, where he encountered 'desert princes and rival sheikhs, blazing with jewel-hilted swords'.

During these extraordinary adventures he was assiduously exploring the desert regions bordering the Nile and patiently recording the antiquities and peoples with his camera. He was the first photographer to venture beyond the sixth cataract. Africa was still the mysterious 'Dark Continent', and Stanley and Livingstone's historic meeting was a decade into the future. The conditions for picture taking confound belief. He laboured for hours in his wicker dark-room in the sweltering heat of the desert, while the volatile chemicals fizzed dangerously in their trays. Often he was forced to work in remote tombs and caves

where conditions were cooler. Back in London he exhibited his photographs and was 'rapturously cheered' by members of the Royal Society. His reputation as a photographer was made overnight. An eminent modern historian has likened their impact on the population of the time to that on our own generation of the first photographs taken on the surface of the moon.

VENTURE OF A LIFE-TIME

Characteristically, Frith quickly spotted the opportunity to create a new business as a specialist publisher of photographs. He lived in an era of immense and sometimes violent change. For the poor in the early part of Victoria's reign work was a drudge and the hours long, and people had precious little free time to enjoy themselves.

Most had no transport other than a cart or gig at their disposal, and had not travelled far beyond the boundaries of their own town or village. However, by the 1870s, the railways had threaded their way across the country, and Bank Holidays and half-day Saturdays had been made obligatory by Act of Parliament. All of a sudden the ordinary working man and his family were able to enjoy days out and see a little more of the world.

With characteristic business acumen, Francis Frith foresaw that these new tourists would enjoy having souvenirs to commemorate their days out. In 1860 he married Mary Ann Rosling and set out with the intention of photographing every city, town and village in Britain. For the next thirty years he travelled the country by train and by pony and trap, producing fine photographs of seaside resorts and beauty spots that were keenly bought by millions of Victorians. These prints were painstakingly pasted into family albums and pored over during the dark nights of winter, rekindling precious memories of summer excursions.

THE RISE OF FRITH & CO

Frith's studio was soon supplying retail shops all over the country. To meet the demand he gathered about him a small team of photographers, and published the work of independent artist-photographers of the calibre of Roger Fenton and Francis Bedford. In order to gain some understanding of the scale of Frith's business one only has to look at the catalogue issued by Frith & Co in 1886: it runs to some 670

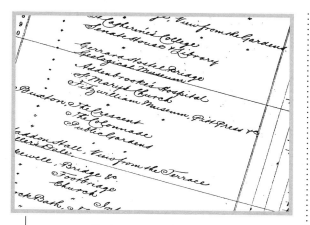

pages, listing not only many thousands of views of the British Isles but also many photographs of most European countries, and China, Japan, the USA and Canada – note the sample page shown above from the hand-written *Frith & Co* ledgers detailing pictures taken. By 1890 Frith had created the greatest specialist photographic publishing company in the world, with over 2,000 outlets – more than the combined number that Boots and WH Smith have today! The picture on the right shows the *Frith & Co* display board at Ingleton in the Yorkshire Dales. Beautifully constructed with mahogany frame and gilt inserts, it could display up to a dozen local scenes.

POSTCARD BONANZA

The ever-popular holiday postcard we know today took many years to develop. In 1870 the Post Office issued the first plain cards, with a pre-printed stamp on one face. In 1894 they allowed other publishers' cards to be sent through the mail with an attached adhesive halfpenny stamp. Demand grew rapidly, and in 1895 a new size of postcard was permitted called the

court card, but there was little room for illustration. In 1899, a year after Frith's death, a new card measuring 5.5 x 3.5 inches became the standard format, but it was not until 1902 that the divided back came into being, with address and message on one face and a full-size illustration on the other. *Frith & Co* were in the vanguard of postcard development, and Frith's sons Eustace and Cyril continued their father's monumental task, expanding the number of views offered to the public and recording more and more places in Britain, as the coasts and countryside were opened up to mass travel.

Francis Frith died in 1898 at his villa in Cannes, his great project still growing. The archive he created continued in business for another seventy years. By 1970 it contained over a third of a million pictures of 7,000 cities, towns and villages. The massive photographic record Frith has left to us stands as a living monument to a special and very remarkable man.

Frith's Archive: *A Unique Legacy*

FRANCIS FRITH'S legacy to us today is of immense significance and value, for the magnificent archive of evocative photographs he created provides a unique record of change in 7,000 cities, towns and villages throughout Britain over a century and more. Frith and his fellow studio photographers revisited locations many times down the years to update their views, compiling for us an enthralling and colourful pageant of British life and character.

We tend to think of Frith's sepia views of Britain as nostalgic, for most of us use them to conjure up memories of places in our own lives with which we have family associations. It often makes us forget that to Francis Frith they were records of daily life as it was actually being lived in the cities, towns and villages of his day. The Victorian age was one of great and often bewildering change for ordinary people, and though the pictures evoke an impression of slower times, life was as busy and hectic as it is today.

We are fortunate that Frith was a photographer of the people, dedicated to recording the minutiae of everyday life. For it is this sheer wealth of visual data, the painstaking chronicle of changes in dress, transport, street layouts, buildings, housing, engineering and landscape that captivates us so much today. His remarkable images offer us a powerful link with the past and with the lives of our ancestors.

TODAY'S TECHNOLOGY

Computers have now made it possible for Frith's many thousands of images to be accessed almost instantly. In the Frith archive today, each photograph is carefully 'digitised' then stored on a CD Rom. Frith archivists can locate a single photograph amongst thousands within seconds. Views can be catalogued and sorted under a variety of categories of place and content to the immediate benefit of researchers. Inexpensive reference prints can be created for them at the touch of a mouse button, and a wide range of books and other printed materials assembled and published for a wider, more general readership - in the next twelve months over a hundred Frith local history titles will be published! The

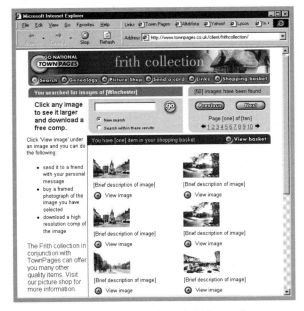

See Frith at www. francisfrith.co.uk

day-to-day workings of the archive are very different from how they were in Francis Frith's time: imagine the herculean task of sorting through eleven tons of glass negatives as Frith had to do to locate a particular sequence of pictures! Yet the archive still prides itself on maintaining the same high standards of excellence laid down by Francis Frith, including the painstaking cataloguing and indexing of every view.

It is curious to reflect on how the internet now allows researchers in America and elsewhere greater instant access to the archive than Frith himself ever enjoyed. Many thousands of individual views can be called up on screen within seconds on one of the Frith internet sites, enabling people living continents away to revisit the streets of their ancestral home town, or view places in Britain where they have enjoyed holidays. Many overseas researchers welcome the chance to view special theme selections, such as transport, sports, costume and ancient monuments.

We are certain that Francis Frith would have heartily approved of these modern developments, for he himself was always working at the very limits of Victorian photographic technology.

THE VALUE OF THE ARCHIVE TODAY

Because of the benefits brought by the computer, Frith's images are increasingly studied by social historians, by researchers into genealogy and ancestory, by architects, town planners, and by teachers and schoolchildren involved in local history projects. In addition, the archive offers every one of us a unique opportunity to examine the places where we and our families have lived and worked down the years. Immensely successful in Frith's own era, the archive is now, a century and more on, entering a new phase of popularity.

THE PAST IN TUNE WITH THE FUTURE

Historians consider the Francis Frith Collection to be of prime national importance. It is the only archive of its kind remaining in private ownership and has been valued at a million pounds. However, this figure is now rapidly increasing as digital technology enables more and more people around the world to enjoy its benefits.

Francis Frith's archive is now housed in an historic timber barn in the beautiful village of Teffont in Wiltshire. Its founder would not recognize the archive office as it is today. In place of the many thousands of dusty boxes containing glass plate negatives and an all-pervading odour of photographic chemicals, there are now ranks of computer screens. He would be amazed to watch his images travelling round the world at unimaginable speeds through network and internet lines.

The archive's future is both bright and exciting. Francis Frith, with his unshakeable belief in making photographs available to the greatest number of people, would undoubtedly approve of what is being done today with his lifetime's work. His photographs, depicting our shared past, are now bringing pleasure and enlightenment to millions around the world a century and more after his death.

EAST ANGLIA – *An Introduction*

OVER THE centuries, East Anglia has managed to keep itself at a distance from the rest of the country without becoming totally isolated. While the character of many other parts of the country changed radically during the 19th century, East Anglia has preserved much of its landscape, architecture and tradition. The only notable change produced by the Industrial Revolution was the coming of the railway, and that helped to spawn a new industry - tourism.

Perhaps it was the relative isolation that produced people who have always been formidable. Queen Boudicca (Boadicea) and her Iceni kept the Roman invaders at bay for some time before being defeated, and Hereward the Wake held out against the Norman invasion from his base in the Fens for five years! Five hundred years later, it took a professional army of twelve thousand to put down the rebellion of Robert Kett and his followers.

Indeed, the East Anglians have had their share of oppression. The Danish raids up to the time of the Conquest were particularly savage and brutal. King Edmund tried to make peace with the Danes by giving himself up, in the hope that the slaughter would cease. Instead, the Danes tortured and murdered him. Take a look at a map, and you'll find many place names with Danish influences - 'toft', 'thorpe' and 'thwaite'. It was King Alfred of Wessex who allowed the Danes to settle in East Anglia.

Of all the famous East Anglians throughout the ages, the most notable has to be the son of a Norfolk rector who became a sailor, despite the fact that he suffered from sea sickness. Horatio Nelson became arguably England's greatest hero. Born in North Norfolk in 1758, he was educated in North Walsham and Norwich, and in 1771 he joined HMS Raisonable. Seven years later, he was semi-retired and living on half pay in Burnham Thorpe with his wife, Fanny. He spent the next five years farming thirty acres of glebe land, and visiting his various relatives throughout the county.

He was appointed Captain of HMS Agamemnon on the outbreak of war in 1793, and a large proportion of his crew were Norfolk men. He held a party at his local pub in Burnham Thorpe (it was the Plough in his day - now, not unexpectedly, it's the Lord

Nelson) before setting off for the Mediterranean. The next twelve years saw Nelson making his mark as England's greatest sailor, inflicting crushing defeats on Napoleon at the Battle of the Nile, the Battle of Copenhagen, and, despite losing his life, at the Battle of Trafalgar in 1805.

The region's name is derived from the land of the East Angles. Similarly, Norfolk and Suffolk originated from 'North Folk' and 'South Folk', while Essex comes from 'East Saxons'. Today, East Anglia is generally regarded as encompassing the four counties of Norfolk, Suffolk, Cambridgeshire - which since the boundary changes of 1974 includes

there are many places where wildlife takes precedence.

Nature conservation has a special home in East Anglia. It was in Norfolk that the first of the County Naturalists Trusts was formed with the purchase of Cley marshes in 1926. The East Anglian reserves offer some of the most varied wildlife habitats in Britain, and the richness of the flora and fauna is beyond compare. The wetland regions of the Broads and the Fens are host to several internationally important wildlife reserves, and the coastal regions have some of the finest salt-marshes and mudflats.

Around the coast, the shifting sand and

Huntingdonshire and the Soke of Peterborough - and Essex.

Since the last war, massive changes have taken place in the countryside of East Anglia. That which is not already under bricks and mortar is now cultivated, either for agriculture or forestry. Most of the old 'unimproved' grasslands, heaths and marshes have fallen to the plough, and hundreds of miles of hedgerow have been ripped out to enlarge fields for modern arable farming. Even so,

shingle and the saltmarshes made agriculture impractical. The sensitive nature of much of the coast precludes that anyway, and with forecasts of rising sea levels, these are likely to be the first areas to see change. The consequences will certainly be nothing new. Coastal towns have been claimed by the sea in the past - Dunwich and much of Aldeburgh, for example - and even today, it continues to nibble away around the North Norfolk coast.

As it is, the balance often seems fragile. It

only takes a combination of spring and high tides with high winds, and the resultant surges can be devastating. The most destructive in recent times was in January 1953, when over 300 square miles of East Anglia was inundated by the sea, and a similar number of people lost their lives.

The East Anglian link with the Dutch lies not only in the similarity of landscapes. In medieval times, the backbone of industry in the area was the wool and cloth-weaving trade. Many Dutch and Flemish weavers settled here when sheep farming was at its height, and created a wool industry which became world-famous. As a result, many buildings in East Anglia have a pronounced Dutch influence.

But mechanisation had its effects then as now. The weaving trade started to decline as long ago as the 16th century. When the first power looms were invented - devices relying on fast running water to provide the power - the textile industry moved north to the Pennines, and when coal became the fuel for industry in the 19th century, the textile factories were already well placed to utilise it.

In the 17th century, more Dutch settlers had arrived to master-mind the incredible feat of engineering which led to the draining of the Fens. The Dutch, of course, are renowned masters of land reclamation, since the greater part of their own country lies below sea level!

Of all the things which might be described as characteristic of East Anglia, the windmill has to be at the top of the list. Wind power, readily available on open land, has been used both for corn milling and drainage in the low-lying parts of Fenland and Broadland. Windmills were actually an Arab invention,

the idea brought over in the 12th century by returning crusaders. None, however, has survived from that period. The earliest still in existence is Bourn mill, in Cambridgeshire, which dates from 1636.

Churches in East Anglia give a fascinating insight into the past and the people who built them. Visitors to the tiny village in Norfolk which gave its name to worsted cloth may wonder where the connection is, until they see the size of the church. Many villages and towns in East Anglia celebrated their prosperity from wool in this way; building and decorating their churches undoubtedly eased their consciences.

They are also as good an example as any that the area is somewhat limited in its choice of building materials. The chalk band which runs across the south of England from the Berkshire Downs to north-west Norfolk is rich in flint. The early settlers were quick to find it, although its use was confined more to making tools and weapons. One of their mines can still be seen at Grimes Graves, near Weeting in Norfolk. The vast majority of churches, too, were built of flint, the poorer parishes making their towers round, in order not to use so much of the precious material. The first buildings made from flint merely had the stones embedded in mortar. Later, the flints were split, so that a wall with a (relatively) flat face could be made, and the different shades of colour could be used to produce patterns.

The very rich, of course, imported their building materials from afar, with stone brought down from the north, or, in the case of Norwich Cathedral, shipped from France. For this reason, most of the large buildings were erected on or near rivers with access to the sea. In parts of west Norfolk, there are also buildings made from a dark brown stone called carr-stone, but its use is not that widespread. In Suffolk, in Lavenham and Kersey, for example, there are many towns and villages with Tudor wood-framed buildings. The more elaborate ones have carved woodwork, and pargetting (moulded plasterwork) for the infill.

Look at any of the small groups of old cottages in an East Anglian village, and the chances are that you will find a pond nearby. It would have been made as a result of villagers excavating material to make the clay lump walls for their timber-framed cottages. There are many fine examples, too, of thatched roofs, demonstrating a craft which has survived the centuries. Norfolk reed is undeniably the best thatching material available, outlasting a wheat straw roof by a good thirty years. Harvested in the Broadland fens, it is still sent far and wide to re-thatch buildings all over the country.

Many towns and villages around the East Anglian coast were once ports for sea or river trade. Coastal erosion and longshore drift closed all but the very best placed sea and estuary ports. Of the smaller ports, whose existence depended on river trade, the vast majority fell into disuse as the draughts of boats became larger. The introduction of railways in the last century was the final nail in their coffin.

The past shouts its presence throughout the region. Colchester is England's oldest recorded town, with many of the old walls and buildings still intact. There is a wealth of Norman architecture, mainly in churches, but also in a few castles and other buildings, not generally so well preserved. Norwich Cathedral is a fine example, as is the castle, although both have had additions over the ages.

Perhaps one of the most heartening aspects as you browse through these pages is the fact that most of the places pictured are still recognisable today. Yes, there have been 'developments' and 'regeneration', but on the whole, the buildings and landscapes which survived the first hundred years of photography are still here to be appreciated.

ESSEX

MALDON
The Promenade 1909 62098

COLCHESTER, HEAD STREET 1891 28212
An empty and rather wintry looking street scene. The road follows the line of the old Roman road which linked
North Gate and Head Gate, both entrance points to the original Roman walled town.

COLCHESTER, ST BOTOLPH'S PRIORY 1892 31528
The overgrown remains of St Boltolph's Priory, a Norman church standing outside the old Roman walls of
Colchester. In about 1100, the priory became the first in the country founded by Augustinian Order. The siege
during the Civil War took its toll, and now only the west front and part of the nave survive.

COLCHESTER, HIGH STREET AND THE TOWN HALL 1901 47650
The impressive Victoria Tower of the Town Hall rises to a height of 162 feet. At the top is a statue of St Helena, Colchester's patron saint, while lowerdown are statues of Queen Boadicea and King Edward the Elder.

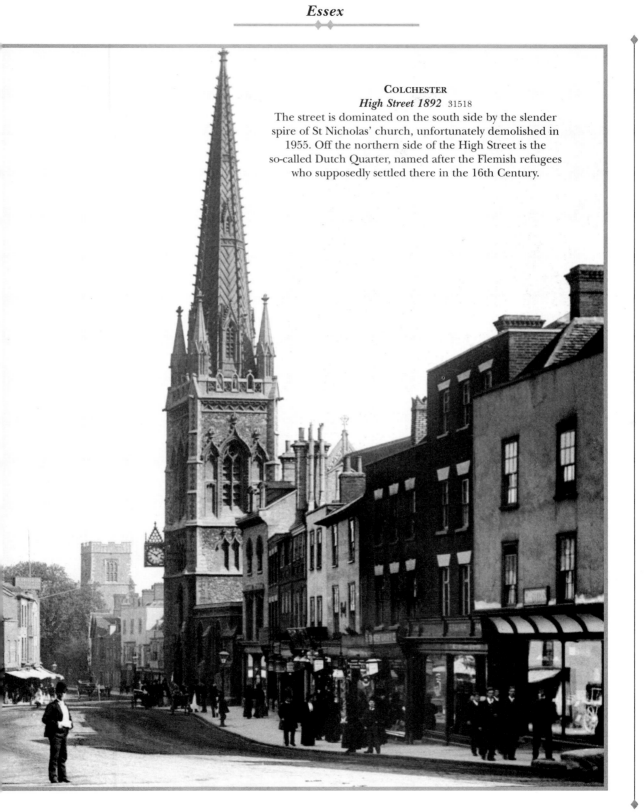

COLCHESTER
High Street 1892 31518
The street is dominated on the south side by the slender spire of St Nicholas' church, unfortunately demolished in 1955. Off the northern side of the High Street is the so-called Dutch Quarter, named after the Flemish refugees who supposedly settled there in the 16th Century.

COLCHESTER, PARK LAKE 1921 70369

The ornamental lake in Lower Castle Park. The profusion of lily pads suggests that its role as a boating lake has not yet been realised.

COLCHESTER, VINEYARD STREET 1904 52348

One row of houses further on is the line of the old Roman wall, whilst just off-camera to the right are the ruins of the Norman St Botolph's Priory, the first in the country founded by the Augustinian Order.

CLACTON-ON-SEA
Electric Parade 1913
As the town's popularity as a holiday resort grew, Victorian streets and shops spread back from the sea. Here were grocers, outfitters, tobacconists and souvenir and fancy goods shops. In this photograph, the awnings are out and the woman in the foreground is sheltering from the hot sun under her dark parasol.

◆

CLACTON-ON-SEA
The Bandstand and Pier 1907
The bandstand on the left would have been the scene for many entertainments for holidaymakers. The pier, opened in 1872, offered a variety of attractions, as well as a good spot for fishermen.

CLACTON-ON-SEA, ELECTRIC PARADE 1913 65239

CLACTON-ON-SEA, THE BANDSTAND AND PIER 1907 58934

CLACTON-ON-SEA, WEST BEACH 1912 64254
Industry and leisure mix in this beach scene. In the foreground are Thames barges with their characteristic lee-
boards - a form of offset keel which can be raised in shallow waters. Behind, rows of bathing machines are ready
to wheel modest bathers down to the water's edge.

CLACTON-ON-SEA, THE BANDSTAND 1907 58935
In Victorian and Edwardian times, when most seaside resorts came into being, part of the entertainment would
involve listening to musicians performing in specially constructed bandstands, like this one on the promenade.

CLACTON-ON-SEA, THE ROYAL HOTEL 1912 64239

It is a hot day. The shop awnings are down and the men are wearing their boaters. Smartly-dressed holidaymakers are wandering up the slope from the Promenade, perhaps to take a genteel cup of tea at the Royal Hotel. Its elegant balconies will ensure airy views of the sea.

BRAINTREE, HIGH STREET 1906 55533

Braintree came into being from its position along the ancient route of pilgrimage from London to Bury St Edmunds and Walsingham, thus establishing a tradition of comfortable inns and hostels, including the Horn Hotel.

BRAINTREE, MARKET SQUARE 1900 46244

Apart from its role as a 'stopover' for pilgrims on their way to Bury St Edmunds or Walsingham, Braintree also had an important role in the East Anglian textile industry, first producing heavy broadcloth, and later the light cloth which took its name from neighbouring Bocking.

SUFFOLK

IPSWICH, BUTTER MARKET 1893 32204
Here, on the corner with St Stephens Lane, stands the Ancient House. This remarkable building was, and still is, probably the best surviving example of medieval pargetting - decorative plasterwork - in Britain.

IPSWICH, THE LOCK GATES 1921 70413
A sailing barge negotiates the lock gates. When the Wet Dock was constructed in Ipswich between 1839 and 1842, it was the most revolutionary and the biggest of its kind in the country.

IPSWICH, TAVERN STREET 1896 37306
Looking east along Tavern Street from Cornhill. On the left is the red brick and stone Lloyds Bank building, with its fretted skyline, while to the right is the neo-classical Post Office, built in 1881. Tavern Street is home to the Great White Horse, an inn stayed in by Charles Dickens, and described by him in 'The Pickwick Papers'.

IPSWICH, THE DOCKS 1893 32208
Situated at the head of the Orwell Estuary, Ipswich has been a major port for centuries. When this picture was taken, the port was starting to enjoy commercial success after two centuries of decline.

BECCLES, FROM THE MARSHES 1894 33332

The River Waveney has been the making of Beccles. In the days when trading wherries plied their way up and down the rivers, transporting goods from the sea ports, or from one town to another, Beccles was a thriving port.

BECCLES, THE MARKET PLACE 1894 33334

Beccles would still have been doing important business as a port when this photograph was taken. The main claim to fame of the church in the background is that Nelson's parents were married there.

BECCLES, THE NEW MARKET C1955 B45045

BECCLES
The New Market c1955

Sixty years on, Beccles has declined as a port, with goods being carried more by road. The church is unusual in that the 92 feet high tower is actually separate from the nave.

◆

BURY ST EDMUNDS
Crown Street 1929

The 15th century St Mary's church is the burial place of Mary Tudor, sister of Henry VIII, and noted for its decorated 'Angel Roof' nave. On the junction with Westgate Street is the Theatre Royal, one of only three surviving Regency theatres in the country, built in 1819 by William Wilkins, architect of the National Gallery. The theatre is famous as being the scene of the world premiere of 'Charley's Aunt' in 1892.

BURY ST EDMUNDS, CROWN STREET 1929 81935

BURY ST EDMUNDS
The Market Place 1898 41246
The original market place, as laid out in the Bury St Edmunds' grid pattern devised by Abbot Baldwin in the 11th century, was a good deal larger than it was by the time of this photograph. Market stalls became permanent over the years, and ended up as two complete rows of buildings. Here, a few street vendors have set out their stalls.

BURY ST EDMUNDS, THE MARKET PLACE c1955 B258003

This photograph shows Angel Hill. Once used as the site of Bury Fair, even by 1955 it had been relegated to a car park. The Angel Hotel which gave its name to the square was immortalised by Charles Dickens in 'The Pickwick Papers'.

NEWMARKET, THE GRAND STAND 1922 71932

Newmarket is the world's capital of horse racing. The Newmarket connection with racing dates back to the time of Charles II, although the sport's main boost came during the reign of Victoria, promoted by her son, the Prince of Wales.

Newmarket, High Street 1922 71914

This street, broad and uncluttered by traffic, is lined with Georgian and Victorian houses, and dominated by the splendid Victorian clock tower at the far end.

Newmarket, Horses at Exercise 1929 81964

Every approach to Newmarket passes through the surrounding heaths, where each day lines of slim, graceful racehorses can be seen being exercised by stable lads.

SUDBURY
The Market 1904 51156
Georgian buildings line Market Hill, with St Peter's
Church at the top. The artist Thomas
Gainsborough was born in Sudbury in a former
16th century inn, and he lived and worked here for
many years.

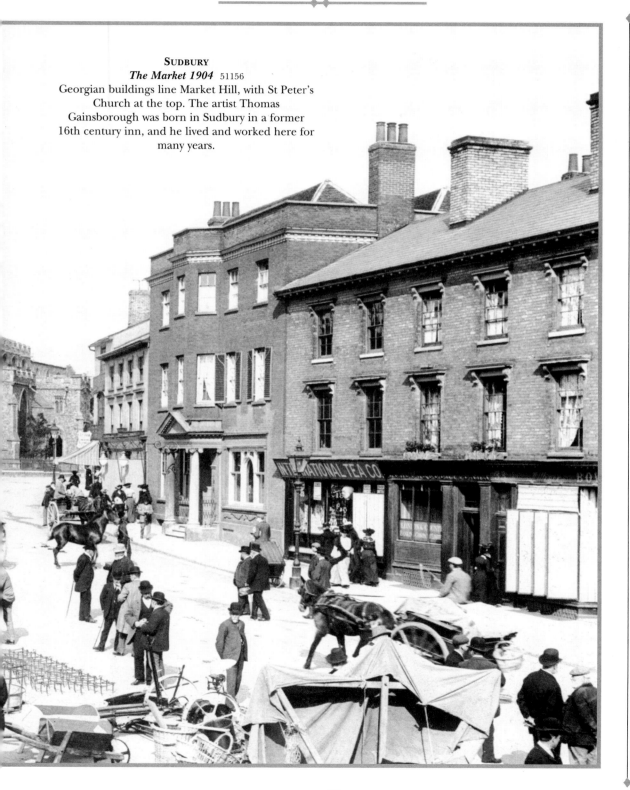

SUDBURY, THE RIVER 1895 35486
Enjoying a stroll along the riverside path beside the Stour. Not far from here are some half-timbered houses dating back to the time when Sudbury was one of the most important weaving towns.

LOWESTOFT, THE PIER FROM THE SANDS 1896 37936

At this time, close to the end of the Victorian era, staying fully clothed on the beach was very much the norm, with sand castles and donkey rides the prime amusements for the children; the adults relax in deck chairs, and shelter from the wind behind umbrellas. Lowestoft can be bracing any time of year...

LOWESTOFT, THE YACHT BASIN 1896 37939

The growth of Lowestoft in Victorian times was largely down to construction by the civil engineer Samuel Morton Peto, who lived in nearby Somerleyton Hall. He was also involved with the building of Nelson's Column, the Houses of Parliament, and railway lines all over the world.

LOWESTOFT, LONDON ROAD 1896 37924
Solid Victorian architecture in this tree-lined road. Like Yarmouth, Lowestoft is a mixture of fishing port and seaside resort; holiday-makers came here as the result of the arrival of the railway in the mid 19th century.

LOWESTOFT, THE HIGH LIGHTHOUSE 1921 71705
Lowestoft is the most easterly point of Britain, with many dangerous sandbanks offshore. Trinity House built two lighthouses, one on the clifftop, one on the shingle below. The present High Light, pictured here, dates back to 1676, and was originally coal-fired. In front of it is a tank from the Great War.

LOWESTOFT, THE PIER PAVILION 1896 37937
Lowestoft's Claremont pier was not built until 1903 - prior to that, the southern breakwater of the harbour built by Samuel Morton Peto was adapted as a pier, giving visitors the contrast of fishing harbour on one side, and beach on the other.

ALDEBURGH, THE MOOT HALL 1894 33360

These days, the timber-framed Tudor Moot Hall (moot is Old English for meeting) stands next to the beach. When it was built, it was right in the centre of town. At the time of this photograph, coastal erosion hasn't yet come that close to the building.

ALDEBURGH, HIGH STREET 1894 33362

The poet George Crabbe was born in Aldeburgh in 1754. His poem about the embittered fisherman Peter Grimes inspired an opera by a much later and better known resident, Benjamin Britten. Just 14 years after this photograph was taken, Elizabeth Garrett Anderson, the first woman Doctor of Medicine, became first woman mayor of an English borough when she took up office in Aldeburgh in 1908.

ALDEBURGH, THE LIFEBOAT 'WINCHESTER' 1903 50426
Aldeburgh lifeboats have always been launched straight from the shingle beach. Four years earlier, an Aldeburgh lifeboat suffered its worst disaster, capsizing with the loss of seven lives.

ALDEBURGH, THE BEACH 1906 5681
Edwardian bathers enjoy the beach. The ever-changing coastline has very much dictated the fortunes of the town, but constant throughout has been the livelihood of the local fishermen, whose boats are parked along the shingle bank.

ALDEBURGH, THE STEPS 1906 56826
The main area of activity in Aldeburgh is the High Street, and from here the Town Steps lead off up a steep hill. Here, grand houses enjoyed a superb view overlooking the town and coastline below.

ALDEBURGH, THE PARADE 1909 62011
Holidaymakers enjoy a stroll. On the right is a lookout tower and boat house for one of Aldeburgh's two lifeboats. The other is just to its left in the distance.

FELIXSTOWE, THE VILLAGE 1899 43246
At this time, Felixstowe enjoyed popularity as a seaside resort, but the dream of eccentric local landowner Colonel Tomline to transform the town into a major port had not yet materialised - that was to take another fifty years! Here, in old Felixstowe, the occasional pony and trap seems to be the only concession to heavy traffic.

FELIXSTOWE
From the Beach 1899 44513
By this time, Felixstowe was at the height of its popularity
as a seaside resort, with its south-facing beach. Of course,
in Victorian times, bathing machines were the order of
the day, and even on the beach, a strict sense of decorum
was maintained.

FELIXSTOWE, RIDES ALONG THE FRONT 1907 58978
Seaside entertainment at Felixstowe had not yet progressed to the garishly commercialised pursuits of today.
Donkey rides were a traditional favourite, along with rides in carriages pulled by goats.

FELIXSTOWE, THE PROMENADE 1904 51251
This view looks north along the Promenade. Although already developed as a port, it was primarily the railway
which brought holidaymakers to enjoy the town as a seaside resort.

FELIXSTOWE, THE DOCKS 1907 58986

When local landowner Colonel Tomline promoted a railway and a new dock in Felixstowe, he hoped to be able to compete with the port of Harwich, across the Orwell Estuary. The dock did not succeed until long after his death, but the railway meantime stimulated the development of Felixstowe as a seaside resort.

FELIXSTOWE, THE PIER 1906 54640

Known more these days as a container port, Felixstowe in 1906 was a genteel seaside resort, and steamers would have pulled up at the pier bringing passengers from Great Yarmouth, Walton-on-the-Naze, Clacton, and even London.

WOODBRIDGE, THE PROMENADE 1906 53495
The bank of the river Deben. Just to the right of the sailing barge is Woodbridge tide mill, the later model of a tide mill which has stood here since the early 12th century.

WOODBRIDGE, THE THOROUGHFARE 1894 33374
Georgian buildings abound in the town, although it harks back to Tudor times, owing much of its early development to Thomas Seckford, a lawyer at the court of Elizabeth I.

NORFOLK

NORWICH, PULLS FERRY 1891 28157
Down river from Bishop's Bridge in Norwich is Pull's Ferry, a 15th century water-gate. It was built on the spot where the specially dug canal for transporting stone for Norwich Cathedral - brought across from Normandy by Bishop Herbert de Losinga - joined the river.

NORWICH, BER STREET 1891 28162
This photograph shows a mixed bag of buildings, many of which have since come down in the course of development. One constant remains at the end of the street, sitting on its junction with Timberhill and Cattlemarket Street - St John Timberhill Church.

NORWICH, PRINCE OF WALES ROAD 1896 37362
Splendid Georgian buildings line the road. On the right is Agricultural Hall, built in 1882, in more recent years used as the city's main post office, and now as the headquarters of Anglia Television.

NORWICH
Cow Tower 1891

Cow Tower was built on the River Wensum in 1378 as a boom tower, controlling the flow of river traffic at the point where the city wall ended. It is the oldest surviving brick building in Norwich, and is reputedly haunted by Old Blunderhazard, a ghostly rider who gallops past on Christmas Eve.

NORWICH
The Guildhall 1891

This fine flint building was built using forced labour in the 15th century. Part of it was used as a prison, and played its part as 'Death Row' to such prisoners as Thomas Bilney, the Tudor heretic, and Robert Kett, the famous Norfolk rebel.

In 1891 it was the seat of local government. Nine years later it was almost demolished, but was saved by the mayor's casting vote.

NORWICH, COW TOWER 1891   28158

NORWICH, THE GUILDHALL 1891   28164

NORWICH
The Cattle Market and the Castle 1891 28177
The Cattle Market stands next to the old Norman castle.
This is where the livestock trade for the area was conducted,
although recently, after many years as nothing more than a
car park, the site was excavated for its archaeological value,
and then turned into a multi-storey underground shopping
precinct called the Castle Mall.

NORWICH, THE MARKET PLACE 1891 29133

One of the largest markets in the country, looking across to the church of St Peter Mancroft. one of the largest and most impressive parish churches in England. With a fine peal of bells, St Peter Mancroft is the resting place of Sir Thomas Browne, the physician whose 'Urn Burial' and 'Religio Medici' are acknowledged prose masterpieces.

NORWICH, ELM HILL 1929 81805

This street was named after an elm tree just up the quaintly cobbled street round to the left. The street contains a variety of old buildings, from Tudor to Georgian.

NORWICH, THE RIVER AT THORPE ST ANDREW 1919 69075

This is the River Yare. While Norwich has operated as a port for hundreds of years, it is only in more recent years that the recreational aspect has become more important, although it is known that Nelson almost certainly learned to sail here.

ACLE, THE RIVER AND RIVER WALK C1929 A204030
Holidays on the Broads were already big business when this photograph of cruisers was taken of the moorings near Acle.

ACLE, FISHING AT ACLE BRIDGE C1929 A204037
Acle lies on the main road between Norwich and Yarmouth. The old bridge had something of a reputation for being haunted. It was the scene of many grisly executions in former times, where hapless criminals were hanged from the parapet and left to rot.

COLTISHALL, THE CORNFIELD 1902 48127
A farm worker and child standing in a freshly harvested cornfield. In the background is the River Bure, which flows into the sea at Great Yarmouth, and which here is the limit of navigation for larger Broads vessels.

COLTISHALL, THE OLD MILL 1902 48149
A wherry loads up at the mill. In these days, square-rigged trading wherries such as this one plied the Broadland waterways carrying all manner of goods, from grain and flour to coal and timber.

COLTISHALL, THE VILLAGE 1902 48166

Here we can see the River Bure. In the second half of the 19th century, Coltishall was a major wherry building centre, and even at the time this photograph was taken, Allens were turning out the sleekest, fastest wherries on the Broads.

HICKLING GREEN, THE PLEASURE BOAT INN c1955 H307011

A favourite pub for many years, the Pleasure Boat Inn these days is the starting point for a water trail which visits the reed beds which make this part of the Norfolk Broads an important wildlife habitat. Three years after this photograph was taken, Hickling Broad became a National Nature Reserve.

HORNING, THE NORFOLK BROADS 1902 48108
The distinctive large black gaff mainsail of a trading wherry dominates the skyline on the River Bure. Wherries were the workhorse cargo boats, often very fast, with the mast hinged and counterbalanced to pass under the numerous bridges spanning the rivers.

HORNING, THE RIVER 1902 48109
Rowing and sailing boats on the reed-fringed River Bure make a typical scene of Broadland tranquillity. In the background the church tower rises among the leafy summer trees.

HORNING, THE REACH C1965 H116123
It is said that this point on the River Bure has seen various means of crossing from one bank to the other for the last thousand years. At this time, the river could be crossed by a chain-pulled ferry.

HORNING, THE BROADS 1902 48110

HORNING
The Broads 1902
The classic Broads marshland scene with an open-trestle windpump. The low-lying marshes of the Broads were drained by windpumps until the 1940s, when electric pumps took over.

◆

LUDHAM
The Old Mill c1955
By the time this photograph was taken, trading wherries were extinct. A few built for pleasure still sailed the Broadland waterways, such as this one passing Turf Fen windpump on the River Ant near Ludham.

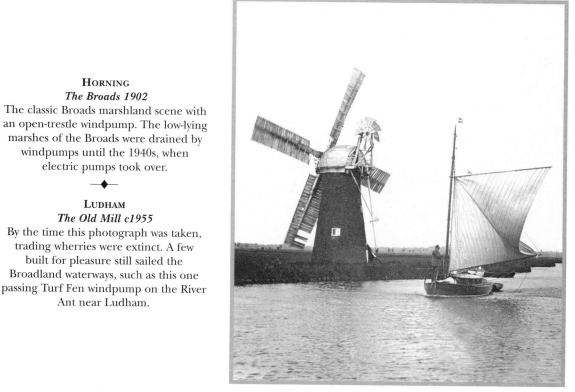

LUDHAM, THE OLD MILL c1955 L110082

LUDHAM, THE VILLAGE c1960 L110030

This village is popular with visitors to Broadland, with St Catherine's church and its beautiful hammer-beam roof and painted rood screen dating from 1493. Not far away are moorings on the River Ant at Ludham Bridge. Holidaymakers on Broads cruisers generally find their way to the King's Arms for their much-needed refreshment.

POTTER HEIGHAM, THE BRIDGE c1926 P167024

Sailing boats on the River Thurne. Unfortunately, the photographer has missed the most attractive thing about this place, the 14th century bridge which is just off the picture to the left. With a headroom of just 7 feet, the stone bridge has been the downfall of many a holiday sailor.

POTTER HEIGHAM, ON THE THURNE c1926 P167040
A pleasure launch on the River Thurne. Holiday cottages line the bank, and in the background is a typical Broadland windpump, used for keeping the surrounding fields drained.

POTTER HEIGHAM, THE FOOT BRIDGE c1955 P167072
While there was still plenty of sailing, by the mid fifties pleasure cruisers were a well-established part of the scenery on Broadland rivers.

GREAT YARMOUTH
The Britannia Pier 1904 52337
Great Yarmouth has two piers, Wellington and Britannia, both
built in the 1850s. The Britannia Pier is at the northern end of
Marine Parade, the main seafront thoroughfare.

GREAT YARMOUTH, BLACKFRIARS TOWER 1891 28710
In medieval times, Great Yarmouth was walled on three sides, with just the river side open. In modern times, long stretches of wall still remain, but before the heavy bombing of the Second World War there would undoubtedly have been more. Blackfriars Tower had a distinctive D-shaped section, and was built around 1340.

GREAT YARMOUTH, THE BEACH 1904 52332
Ever since the arrival of the railway, Great Yarmouth has been a popular seaside resort, and whilst not the quiet getaway some might prefer, it was always a great pull for working class families from London and the Midlands.

GREAT YARMOUTH, THE TOWER 1922 72518
The Tower stood on Marine Parade, but it was demolished at the start of World War II. Visitors would sit on a circular seat and be lifted slowly to the viewing platform, where they could walk about and admire the views over Yarmouth and the surrounding countryside.

GREAT YARMOUTH
The Market 1908 60651
In the distance is St Nicholas's Church, said to be one of the largest
parish churches in England. Just off the far end of the Market Place is
the old Fishermen's Hospital, founded in 1702 for retired fishermen
and their wives.

GREAT YARMOUTH, KING STREET 1896 37957
This is the main shopping street in Great Yarmouth. The most interesting feature of the town is the Rows, enormous numbers of parallel alleys leading off to the west of King Street. There were nearly 150 of them when this photograph was taken - many were destroyed later by World War II bombing.

GREAT YARMOUTH, THE WINTER GARDENS 1908 60650
Here, holidaymakers take a relaxing walk. The gardens embellish the entrance to Wellington Pier, and had been bought at a knockdown price from Torquay, where they had originally been sited from 1878 to 1881.

GORLESTON, THE HARBOUR 1894 33393
These sailing barges in Gorleston Harbour would still have been the mainstay for conveying cargo from one port to another. But just as in this photograph, the big takeover by steam was just around the corner.

GORLESTON, THE PIER 1908 60662
Great Yarmouth and Gorleston share a common harbour entrance. Here, the breakwater on the Gorleston side proves a popular place for holidaymakers to take the sea air and watch the comings and goings of boats in and out of the harbour.

GORLESTON, HIGH STREET 1908 60663
Like its great neighbour, Great Yarmouth, Gorleston grew up in the 19th century. As the town expanded, because of the burgeoning holiday trade, trams were introduced to convey visitors from the seafront to their boarding houses.

GORLESTON, HIGH STREET 1908 60664

Looking east, we can see an electric tram and horse-drawn cart providing an interesting contrast of the old and the new. On the right, a hotel has sprung up and cashed in by calling itself 'The Tramway Hotel'.

GORLESTON, THE SANDS 1896 37974

In Victorian times, the preservation of modesty was paramount, so tents and bathing machines were very much the order of the day to allow bathers to change.

CAISTER-ON-SEA, DONKEY RIDGE c1955 C450081
In the mid 1950's, donkey rides on the beach were all the rage, and these children are enjoying themselves. The trailers in the foreground would be used to launch fishing boats into the sea.

CAISTER-ON-SEA, THE LIFEBOAT c1955 C450112
Caister, just north of Great Yarmouth, has a strong tradition for both fishing and its lifeboat. In 1901, the lifeboat was launched into a storm, and nine out of the twelve crew lost their lives. At the inquiry afterwards, the survivors were asked why they had carried on when conditions made a rescue impossible. Their answer, 'Caister men never turn back', has been the motto of Caister seafarers ever since.

CAISTER-ON-SEA, PLEASURE FLIGHTS c1955 C450300
A short flight in this light aircraft, even just a few hundred feet up, would give the sightseeing holidaymaker a marvellous view of both the coastline and the Broads inland.

DISS, THE MARKET PLACE c1965 D32033
The Market Place contains an interesting architectural mixture of Tudor, Georgian and Victorian buildings. St Mary's church has a fine knapped-flint chancel. One of its past rectors, John Skelton, a Poet Laureate, gave school lessons to the young Henry VIII.

DISS

Mere Street 1925 77324

The original town was built around a six acre lake
called the Mere, its southern edge bordered by a
large village green. The Market Place and Mere
Street contain an interesting architectural mixture -
Tudor, Georgian and Victorian buildings.

GARBOLDISHAM, THE GARAGE c1955 G188027

The tiny village of Garboldisham on the Norfolk / Suffolk border has many houses made of the knapped flint which is so characteristic of the area. Here, the most distinctive element of the photograph is the two tall petrol pumps at the local garage.

GARBOLDISHAM, HARVEST TIME c1955 G188029

While mechanisation had already come into farming by 1955, there were still plenty of places where more traditional practices continued. Here, horse-drawn carts have not yet been usurped by tractors and combine harvesters.

EAST DEREHAM, CHURCH STREET 1893 33303

A solitary pony and trap head down the street. In the churchyard of St. Nicholas' church is the grave of the melancholic poet William Cowper, and St. Withburga's Well, the site of the grave of one of the sainted daughters of the Saxon King Anna.

EAST DEREHAM, BISHOP BONNER'S COTTAGE 1898 42765

This thatched cottage with its distinctive pargetting (moulded plaster decoration) was home to one of East Dereham's more infamous sons, Bishop Bonner, the Rector of nearby St Nicholas' church in the 1530s. As Bishop of London during the reign of Mary Tudor, he earned the name 'Bloody Bonner' for his part in sending so many Protestants to be burned at the stake.

EAST DEREHAM
The Market Place 1898 42759
The market place was once a good deal bigger than
this, but fire swept through the town in 1679, and
subsequent rebuilding encroached on the site. In
the corner is the Corn Hall, built in 1857, with its
impressive Corinthian columns.

DOWNHAM MARKET, DENVER MILL c1965 D149003

DOWNHAM MARKET
Denver Mill c1965

The six storey high Denver windmill was built around 1835. Although Denver is best known for its sluices, which control the drainage of a large part of the surrounding fens, the windmill is not a windpump used for drainage, but a mill for grinding corn.

DOWNHAM MARKET
The Town Hall c1965

A market town situated on the edge of the Fens, Downham Market's buildings are often constructed from carr-stone, an attractive rust-coloured sandstone characteristic of Norfolk. The young Nelson attended the grammar school here.

DOWNHAM MARKET, THE TOWN HALL c1965 D149008

WOLFERTON, THE STATION 1921 71064

After the purchase of Sandringham House, the tiny station at Wolferton became the stopping off point for visiting members of the Royal family. Here they would alight from the train and take refreshments while their luggage was being transported to the house.

WOLFERTON, THE VILLAGE C1955 W354005

Apart from the proximity of the railway station which saw the arrival of Royal visitors on their way to Sandringham, Wolferton was and is now a quiet little village.

SANDRINGHAM HOUSE 1896 38395

Traditionally the gathering place for the Royal family in the New Year, it was originally bought by Queen Victoria as a twenty-first birthday gift for Edward when he was Prince of Wales. Her intention was that he should spend his off-duty time 'away from town.... to enjoy the benefits of a healthy, country life'.

SANDRINGHAM HOUSE FROM THE LAKE c1955 S58029

The estate in which the house stands is very beautiful, its heath and forest land described as a 'piece of Scotland south of the Tweed'.

KING'S LYNN, SOUTHGATE 1891 28760
Seen here at low tide, where Friar's Fleet meets the London Road, the early 16th century Southgate is one of the few remaining sections of King's Lynn's town walls.

KING'S LYNN, HIGH STREET 1891 28770
This late Victorian scene of the High Street typifies a more tranquil era, where the only signs of traffic pollution appear to be from the passing of the pony and trap further down the road!

KING'S LYNN, THE CUSTOM HOUSE 1898 40878
The Custom House was built in the Palladian style in 1683 by Henry Bell, then mayor of this thriving port. Originally intended as an Exchange for local merchants, it became the Custom House in the early 18th century.

KING'S LYNN, TUESDAY MARKET 1898 40886

The Tuesday Market is a grand open space surrounded by a fine mixture of buildings dating from the 17th, 18th and 19th centuries. A market has been held here for hundreds of years, and originally there would have been a pillory and gallows here too.

KING'S LYNN, THE HONEST LAWYER INN 1925 78717

An austere inn, perhaps, but welcoming none the less. The architecture is vaguely Dutch, in line with that of many East Anglian houses, with its double pitch roof.

KING'S LYNN
High Street 1908 60023
Perhaps the most noticeable aspect of the picture is the acute interest being taken by everyone in the scene - of course, in those days, taking a photograph involved considerably more than the point-and-shoot techniques with today's cameras.

HUNSTANTON, TOWN GREEN AND PIER 1907 58894
Hunstanton's chief feature is its distinctive white and red banded cliffs, which rise from nothing at this point to a towering 30 metres just 300 metres further north.

HUNSTANTON, THE PIER 1921 71033
The pier at this popular seaside resort was swept away in gales during the 1970s. Because of its situation on the Wash, Hunstanton is the only east coast resort where you can watch the sun set over the sea!

WELLS-NEXT-THE-SEA
The Quay c1955
This photograph was taken just beyond the East Quay. Just two years earlier, Wells had been one of the worst hit places during the 1953 floods which devastated much of the east coast.

◆

WELLS-NEXT-THE-SEA
Near the Quay c1955
There are several narrow lanes running perpendicular to the quay at Wells. Some of the buildings here would appear to be in need of some maintenance. Looming over the rooftops in the background is the vast bulk of the 19th century granary on the quay.

WELLS-NEXT-THE-SEA, THE QUAY c1955 W48040

WELLS-NEXT-THE-SEA, NEAR THE QUAY c1955 W48049

WELLS-NEXT-THE-SEA, THE QUAY SIDE c1965 W48134
Despite the fact that coastal silt deposits have left Wells Quay on a creek over a mile from the open sea, the port was still functioning for the export of locally grown grain in 1965. In the gales of January 1978, a coaster was lifted onto the quayside itself.

BLAKENEY, THE VILLAGE c1955 B121052
Flint and brick feature predominantly in traditional Norfolk buildings, particularly so in the pretty village of Blakeney, seen here looking down towards the marshes. A sleepy village now, in medieval times Blakeney was one of the top ten ports in England.

BLAKENEY, THE FERRY BOAT c1955 B121054

A ferry boat departing from Blakeney Quay. Sheltering Blakeney from the sea is a 4 mile spit of land called Blakeney Point, a nature reserve since 1912, and home to nesting colonies of terns, oystercatchers and redshanks.

CLEY NEXT THE SEA, THE VILLAGE c1955 C118004

Cley (rhymes with sky), once a busy port, is now a sleepy village, where nothing much has changed since this photograph was taken. The character of the village comes from the distinctive flint and red brick houses with clay pantile roofs.

CLEY NEXT THE SEA
The Windmill 1933 85836

Whilst some parts of the Norfolk coast have suffered
badly from erosion over the years, Cley next the Sea
has suffered from precisely the opposite. In fact,
silting up has put it more than a half a mile from
the sea. This beautiful 18th century windmill once
stood on the quayside of a busy port.

HOLT, THE MARKET PLACE 1896 37977
A great fire destroyed much of the town in 1708, with the result that Holt is principally Georgian in appearance. One of the greatest curiosities in Holt is the so-called Pineapple Obelisk, inscribed with the mileages to several places, correct from Melton Constable Hall, where it originally served as a gatepost, but incorrect for Holt.

HOLT, THE HALL FROM THE LAKE 1896 37985
A picturesque vista of Holt Hall, with its towering chimneys and many gables, cradled in magnificent parkland with shady trees.

FAKENHAM, MARKET SQUARE C1955 F3024

Attractive late 18th and early 19th century buildings can be found around Market Square. Dominating the skyline is the 15th century tower of the church of St Peter and St Paul.

FAKENHAM, THE OLD MILL C1965 F3026

For centuries the town mill had ground the corn for the local farmers. In this photograph we can see a fascinating jumble of building styles - vernacular weatherboarding, Georgian brick, Victorian decorative brickwork and later chimney cowls and other less attractive accretions.

FAKENHAM, NORWICH STREET C1955 F3002
Traffic congestion is still waiting to hit Norwich Street. Even the postman is using a hand-pushed cart to make his deliveries.

MUNDESLEY, HIGH STREET 1921 71010
Looking west along the High Street, we see buildings which are characteristic of North Norfolk: flints set in mortar, with brick facings.

MUNDESLEY, THE PARADE c1965 M109064
On the left is the distant imposing form of the Manor Hotel. Despite the fact that the railway which brought the village resort status in 1898 closed in 1959, Mundesley's quiet popularity has remained.

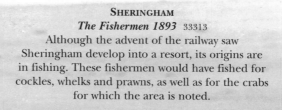

SHERINGHAM
The Fishermen 1893 33313
Although the advent of the railway saw
Sheringham develop into a resort, its origins are
in fishing. These fishermen would have fished for
cockles, whelks and prawns, as well as for the crabs
for which the area is noted.

SHERINGHAM, HIGH STREET 1921 70993
The street is dominated by its distinctive town clock. It is hard to believe that this scene was almost lost some 30 years later in plans to 'reconstruct' the heart of the town. Fortunately they were averted, and the buildings and clock still survive.

SHERINGHAM, FISHERMEN MENDING LOBSTER POTS 1906 56879
The fishermen of Cromer and Sheringham have long been rivals, the Cromer men calling the Sheringhammers 'Shannocks', which may derive from 'shanny', a dialect word meaning unruly. Here, character etched on every face, a group of Sheringham fishermen mend their crab pots ready to be used the next day.

SHERINGHAM 1893 33311

When this photograph was taken, Sheringham was a small fishing village on the north Norfolk coast, noted for its crabs. Throughout the 1890s the village developed into a seaside resort, sparked off by the building of two hotels, the Grand and the Sheringham.

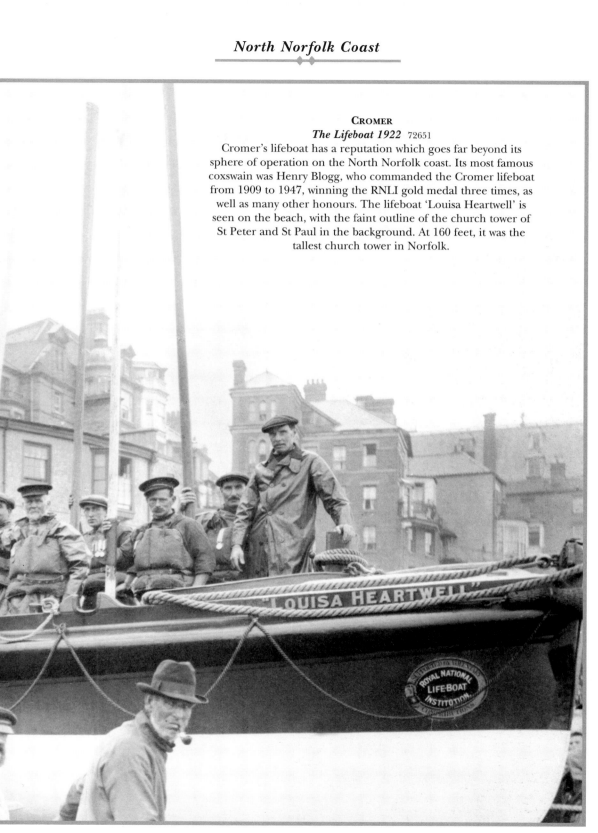

CROMER
The Lifeboat 1922 72651
Cromer's lifeboat has a reputation which goes far beyond its sphere of operation on the North Norfolk coast. Its most famous coxswain was Henry Blogg, who commanded the Cromer lifeboat from 1909 to 1947, winning the RNLI gold medal three times, as well as many other honours. The lifeboat 'Louisa Heartwell' is seen on the beach, with the faint outline of the church tower of St Peter and St Paul in the background. At 160 feet, it was the tallest church tower in Norfolk.

CROMER, THE LIGHTHOUSE 1894 33326
Still relatively new when this photograph was taken, the lighthouse on the cliffs to the east of Cromer replaced an earlier one which fell into the sea. Before that, the town's church tower - the tallest in Norfolk - used to be employed as a lighthouse.

CROMER, GARDEN STREET 1894 33330
Twenty years before this photograph was taken, Cromer was a quiet resort, frequented only by those who sought refuge from the day trippers visiting Great Yarmouth in droves. In the 1880s, Daily Telegraph writer Clement Scott put Cromer on the map as 'Poppyland', and by 1897 a non-stop rail service took visitors from London to Cromer in 175 minutes.

CAMBRIDGESHIRE

CAMBRIDGE, PETTY CURY 1931 84534
The narrow street of Petty Cury runs between Market Hill and Sidney Street. Opposite the east end of Petty Cury is the entrance to Christ College, beyond which are the gardens and mulberry tree under which Milton is said to have written 'Lycidas'.

CAMBRIDGE
The Eights 1909 61510
Cambridge has a long history of rowing. Because the
River Cam itself is not wide enough for conventional
races, races called 'Bumps' are held. Eights such as
this one start off some one and a half lengths behind
one another, and each boat has to catch up with the
one in front, thus "bumping' it.

CAMBRIDGE
Sidney Street 1931 84538
These days, Cambridge streets have become
so congested that parts of the city are no-go
areas for cars. Here, the policeman directing
traffic appears to have an easy job!

CAMBRIDGE, BRIDGE OF SIGHS 1890 26449

Joining the two courts of St John's College on either side of the River Cam is the Bridge of Sighs. It borrows the idea of the covered bridge from the one of the same name in Venice. Although the Cambridge version, built in 1831, has barred unglazed windows, the students passing through it were not necessarily looking their last upon the outside world, as the users of the original were!

HUNTINGDON, MARKET HILL 1901 46620

To the right of the tree is the former Elizabethan grammar school, which has two very famous pupils in its history - the diarist Samuel Pepys, and Oliver Cromwell, MP for Huntingdon and Lord Protector. The building is now a museum devoted to Cromwell and the Civil War.

HUNTINGDON, THE BRIDGE 1898   41251

The medieval bridge over the River Ouse. Its building was begun in 1332 to connect Huntingdon with Godmanchester, and the respective authorities paid for three arches - note the different styles - with the builders starting on each bank and meeting in the middle!

ELY, MARKET PLACE 1925   78276

While the cathedral is the main feature of Ely, it has also been a market town for many years. In this photograph, the Market Place occupies far more space than it does these days.

ELY

Fore Hill 1925 78274

Fore Hill is an attractive street which continues on from the High Street, descending to the River Ouse. Although the town itself is very much low-key compared to the impressive cathedral, it does have its place in folklore, with its association with Hereward the Wake; it is firmly rooted in history by its connection with Oliver Cromwell, for a time Member of Parliament for Ely.

ELY, THE RIVER OUSE C1955   E34014

The rowers pictured here would almost certainly have come from Cambridge University, who tend to use the river here when practising for the Oxford and Cambridge boat race because of its greater width than the River Cam.

ELY, THE CATHEDRAL FROM THE RIVER 1891   28179

Ely Cathedral, living up to its nickname 'the ship of the Fens', floats above the rooftops and surrounding countryside. The 14th century octagonal central tower is a piece of architectural genius - four hundred tons of masonry appear from the inside to be suspended without any apparent means of support.

ELY, THE CATHEDRAL C1878   10955

The west end. The porch is known as the Galilee porch, so called because as Galilee was the furthest place in the Holy Land from Bethlehem, so too is the west porch furthest from the altar.

ELY
Overhead View c1955 E34068

Index

To receive your FREE Mounted Print

Cut out this Voucher and return it with your remittance for £1.50 to cover postage and handling. Choose any photograph included in this book. Your SEPIA print will be A4 in size, and mounted in a cream mount with burgundy rule lines, overall size 14 x 11 inches.

Order additional Mounted Prints at HALF PRICE (only £7.49 each*)

If there are further pictures you would like to order, possibly as gifts for friends and family, acquire them at half price (no additional postage and handling required).

Have your Mounted Prints framed*

For an additional £14.95 per print you can have your chosen Mounted Print framed in an elegant polished wood and gilt moulding, overall size 16 x 13 inches (no additional postage and handling required).

---

* IMPORTANT!

These special prices are only available if ordered using the original voucher on this page (no copies permitted) and at the same time as your free Mounted Print, for delivery to the same address

---

Frith Collectors' Guild

From time to time we publish a magazine of news and stories about Frith photographs and further special offers of Frith products. If you would like 12 months FREE membership, please return this form and we will send you a New Member Pack.

Send completed forms to:
The Francis Frith Collection, Frith's Barn, Teffont, Salisbury, Wiltshire SP3 5QP

Voucher for FREE and Reduced Price Frith Prints

Picture no.	Page number	Qty	Mounted @ £7.49	Framed + £14.95	Total Cost
		1	Free of charge*	£	£
			£	£	£
			£	£	£
			£	£	£
			£	£	£
			£	£	£

Title: EAST ANGLIA
059-4

* Post & handling		£1.50
Total Order Cost		**£**

Please do not photocopy this voucher. Only the original is valid, so please cut it out and return it to us.

I enclose a cheque / postal order for £ . . . .
made payable to 'The Francis Frith Collection'
OR please debit my Mastercard / Visa / Switch / Amex card

Number . . . .

Expires . . . . Signature . . . .

Name Mr/Mrs/Ms . . . .

Address . . . .

. . . .

. . . .

. . . .

. . . . Postcode . . . .

Daytime Tel No . . . .   Valid to 31/12/01

The Francis Frith Collectors' Guild

I would like to receive the New Members Pack offering 12 months FREE membership.

059-4

Name Mr/Mrs/Ms . . . .

Address . . . .

. . . .

. . . .

. . . . Postcode . . . .

Frith Book Co 1999 Titles

From 2000 we aim at publishing 100 new books each year. For latest catalogue please contact Frith Book Co

Barnstaple	1-85937-084-5	£12.99	Oct 99
Blackpool	1-85937-049-7	£12.99	Sep 99
Bognor Regis	1-85937-055-1	£12.99	Sep 99
Bristol	1-85937-050-0	£12.99	Sep 99
Cambridge	1-85937-092-6	£12.99	Oct 99
Cambridgeshire	1-85937-086-1	£14.99	Nov 99
Cheshire	1-85937-045-4	£14.99	Sep 99
Chester	1-85937-090-X	£12.99	Nov 99
Chesterfield	1-85937-071-3	£12.99	Sep 99
Chichester	1-85937-089-6	£12.99	Nov 99
Cornwall	1-85937-054-3	£14.99	Sep 99
Cotswolds	1-85937-099-3	£14.99	Nov 99

Maidstone	1-85937-056-X	£12.99	Sep 99
Northumberland & Tyne and Wear	1-85937-072-1	£14.99	Sep 99
North Yorkshire	1-85937-048-9	£14.99	Sep 99
Nottingham	1-85937-060-8	£12.99	Sep 99
Oxfordshire	1-85937-076-4	£14.99	Oct 99
Penzance	1-85937-069-1	£12.99	Sep 99
Reading	1-85937-087-X	£12.99	Nov 99
St Ives	1-85937-068-3	£12.99	Sep 99
Salisbury	1-85937-091-8	£12.99	Nov 99
Scarborough	1-85937-104-3	£12.99	Sep 99
Scottish Castles	1-85937-077-2	£14.99	Oct 99
Sevenoaks and Tonbridge	1-85937-057-8	£12.99	Sep 99
Sheffield and S Yorkshire	1-85937-070-5	£12.99	Sep 99
Shropshire	1-85937-083-7	£14.99	Nov 99
Southampton	1-85937-088-8	£12.99	Nov 99
Staffordshire	1-85937-047-0	£14.99	Sep 99
Stratford upon Avon	1-85937-098-5	£12.99	Nov 99
Suffolk	1-85937-074-8	£14.99	Oct 99
Surrey	1-85937-081-0	£14.99	Oct 99
Torbay	1-85937-063-2	£12.99	Sep 99
Wiltshire	1-85937-053-5	£14.99	Sep 99

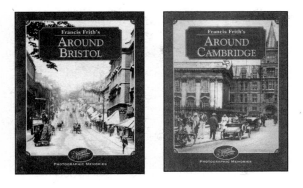

Derby	1-85937-046-2	£12.99	Sep 99
Devon	1-85937-052-7	£14.99	Sep 99
Dorset	1-85937-075-6	£14.99	Oct 99
Dorset Coast	1-85937-062-4	£14.99	Sep 99
Dublin	1-85937-058-6	£12.99	Sep 99
East Anglia	1-85937-059-4	£14.99	Sep 99
Eastbourne	1-85937-061-6	£12.99	Sep 99
English Castles	1-85937-078-0	£14.99	Oct 99
Essex	1-85937-082-9	£14.99	Nov 99
Falmouth	1-85937-066-7	£12.99	Sep 99
Hampshire	1-85937-064-0	£14.99	Sep 99
Hertfordshire	1-85937-079-9	£14.99	Nov 99
Isle of Man	1-85937-065-9	£14.99	Sep 99
Liverpool	1-85937-051-9	£12.99	Sep 99

British Life A Century Ago

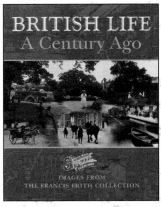

246 x 189mm 144pp, hardback. Black and white Lavishly illustrated with photos from the turn of the century, and with extensive commentary. It offers a unique insight into the social history and heritage of bygone Britain.

1-85937-103-5 £17.99 ....

Available from your local bookshop or from the publisher